To Gabriel!
Love Ryan
You are the
Buddha

Transcending the Illusion of Temporal Limitations

Transcending the Illusion of Temporal Limitations

Ryan H. McJury

iUniverse, Inc.
New York   Bloomington   Shanghai

Transcending the Illusion of Temporal Limitations

Copyright © 2008 by Ryan H. McJury

All rights reserved. No part of this book may be used or reproduced by any means, graphic, electronic, or mechanical, including photocopying, recording, taping or by any information storage retrieval system without the written permission of the publisher except in the case of brief quotations embodied in critical articles and reviews.

iUniverse books may be ordered through booksellers or by contacting:

iUniverse
1663 Liberty Drive
Bloomington, IN 47403
www.iuniverse.com
1-800-Authors (1-800-288-4677)

Because of the dynamic nature of the Internet, any Web addresses or links contained in this book may have changed since publication and may no longer be valid.

The views expressed in this work are solely those of the author and do not necessarily reflect the views of the publisher, and the publisher hereby disclaims any responsibility for them.

ISBN: 978-0-595-46643-6 (pbk)
ISBN: 978-0-595-90938-4 (ebk)

Printed in the United States of America

Escape Velocity—The minimum speed required for a particle, mass, space vehicle, or being to escape permanently from the gravitational field of a planet, star, or galaxy.

You are the only other me …
Since we were here last …
The future is now the present …
And the present is now the past …

—R.H. McJury

You are me I am you

We transcend time and space.
This has always been the case.

At every moment that we face,
There is no other place.

You may be from Sirius C.
You are a planet, a star, and also a tree.

If you look at the sky,
Then you are looking at me.

I am close, yet I'm far.
And I'm as bright as a star.

And if you were to ask,
I'd reveal who you are.

We are all united,
By a certain force,

The stars are a map,
And your life is the course.

And of course,

You may clearly see,
        It's so obvious,
                That you are me.

I am you, and that is true,
        And together we are one.

The unity of being exists in everyone.

Perceiver of the world's sounds

In the lost paths of my mind.
I thought once of time.

I wished all could understand my find.
For they declare, "War!"

"I declare Peace!"
Grateful for everything.

We all know, battlefields flow red.
Yet, is the civilization is illegible to those who bled?

War and violence are like two old worn out shoes
That we have outgrown, as well.

All the peaceful pled …
"We need something, or someone to awaken the people."

The last you built some shelves.

And on those shelves,
You put a bell …

To ring in times of trouble …
In times of great need.

You hear the bell.
You are the bell.

I believe in the vast infinite.
And In the Universal law only.

As a Universal being, and a learner …
I can see, hear, and feel a distant force.

I see, hear, and feel it through distant waves.

"Universal peace! Unity of being!" this force exclaims into infinity …

"We will spread the peace together!" This force and I proclaim, as one.

Then I answer, "Avolokiteshvara, is that you?"

5

Confused, and unconvinced?
Well, you can see it, or you can't.

I can't make you understand,
I can't turn on the lamp.

But, a light, it will come in,
And wake you from your slumber.

You'll awaken, and you'll see,
That nothing is a number.

Nothing is a number,
Just the same as five.

If you look, listen, and feel …
Then you are alive.

The ultimate knowledge,
Is knowing that you know nothing,

Nothing is for certain,
So quit pushing, and shoving.

The only thing that exists,
Is existence itself.

Just because you are rich,
Doesn't mean you have wealth.

I think, therefore I am,
I am, therefore I be.

We exist on a plane,
That is way too high, to see.

Points

A flock of people seek an enlightened "idol" to follow blindly.
They don't understand. Study the teaching. Do not follow blindly.
Enlightenment and wisdom are not outside of your "self".
"Idols" are meant to awaken you to become enlightened yourself,

Some will exploit your thirst for knowledge,
To trick you into believing false ideas, and doctrines.
To further their own causes and efforts of greed and corruption,
They will distort an enlightened being's teachings.

They will try to trick you into wearing the blindfold of the masses,
They prey on your thirst for wisdom by feeding you incorrect teachings,
Sometimes based upon correct teachings, yet distorted.
The truth becomes obscured. Uncover the blindfold by finding the truth.

Stay clear from those who seek to lead you into darkness.
There are correct teachers who teach correct knowledge.
You will know in your heart that which is correct, and that which is not.
Use these as your teacher, though they are not easily sought, and few.

"They are the finger, pointing at the moon.
They are not the moon itself."—Siddhartha Gautama
Maybe a teacher to help you along your path is wise,
But any "idol", to idolize blindly is dangerous.

A teacher may teach you …
Love, peace, kindness, and compassion are their qualities.
Greed, anger, jealousy, arrogance, and ignorance,
Are the traits you must leave behind, as their student.

Violent wars have been fought to preserve peaceful teachings.
And war and violence were in direct contradiction to the teachings.
A contradiction of the worst kind. The ends never justify the means.
The answers are out there, and all radiate love, peace, and compassion.

I learned that love and peace will triumph over war violence.
And even if people have erroneous views, show them respect.
Stand your point true, and hold it.
They will soon realize the truth.

I've defended the street you and I walk freely and peacefully upon.
I wanted to understand a lot of things,
But I was hindered sometimes by blocks.
I tried to find my own way, but I got lost sometimes, too.

A map would have been helpful. But there was no map of life.
So I had to feel my way around, and test the water.

The Sound

A quiet noise is heard by all,
   Who don't incline themselves to listen.

Hear the tree grow,
   But why does no one notice?

A car drove fast, a train traveled faster,
   But the plane is too fast, say I.

Hurry, hurry to your death,
   I stay slow …
            And gather breath.

I sigh.
   Once again, I hear a lie.
      She is the keeper of freedom,
Chained to the night with ceramic shackles.

      Forgotten …
         I Think …

No time to notice.
            Lost dogs cry out for food.
Hunger, starvation,
      Suffering and pain.
           Warring nations.

Fire beneath.
      Us, we, they, them,
           Who?
   Tickle a scripture.
         Interpret a scorpion.

Congratulate her,
     Tell her she is your world,
   Or she will go quietly.
      The noise was fate.

Of choice

Choose another person to decide your fate,
And the fate your planet?

Choose wrong or correct.
Does not matter,

All choices are wrong,
Incorrect.

Navigate the universe together,
We must come together for peace.

Despite the rain,
My emotions are still scarred.

The remedy is a new way,
A peaceful way.

The old way is proven wrong.
The way of war and violence.

I feared this old way,
Of a world dominated by war and violence.

Now, I fear it, no longer.
I vow to fight for peace and unity.

Our liberties are gone.
Our rights are now privileges.

For she is no longer safe.
   Who is she?
      She is freedom.

Taken away, forgotten in an argument of constitutions.
Constitute my love for this earth and the people I share it with.

And share it with me, in return!
Repair your procedures, or establish new ones.

We must protect freedom,
And hold our heads high above the clouds of illusion.

Universal

I'm defining

I'm combining.

I see through the limitless light.

I've been there.

I've seen it.

It's a secret in the night.

They scheme,

And they plot,

There is something you can do.

To end it or expose it …

The peaceful are not few.

We are humble,

We are strong.

In the end we'll be the victor.

The good are good.

The bad are bad.

And I am just a drifter.

Convince me it's not relative,

And I'll convince you it's not real.

I live inside a shadow,

    In a mountain …

        In a field.

I saw a loving sunbeam,

Shining upon the people.

It radiated love,

And freedom was its equal.

It showed a vision …

    Of a lifetime …

        Lost inside a memory.

I live inside a world surreal,

That someone else has lent me.

Untitled

A word in time, in time you'll find,

    Its threat is never ending.

Just lend some time and drop a dime,

    This doesn't count as spending.

Re-arrange the way of all,

    And in the end you'll see.

The one I am,

    The one I is.

        That's all I'll ever be.

Another and another,

    Until all is forgotten?

Exceed your bounds!

    Repair your world!

Before you turn it rotten?

June 1997
For Laura Lynn

I finally met inspiration.

In it's purest form.

Her words stung me.

Like a million bee's swarm.

Beauty all overpowering,

With no lapse of reason,

Then I realized right now,

It is Laura Lynn season.

I thought I had met her, many times before.

I was always wrong,

Then she knocked on my door.

Not even knowing,

That she was the one,

I opened my world to her,

Yet, she was the sun.

All along the lost hallways of time,

I called out,

And was not heard,

Love came near,

And that was the word.

For Laura Lynn

One cent in my pocket divided by two
 Is enough for my need, how about you?

Is a story enough to carry your soul from day, to day,
 Until, we are old?

Will you love my smile?
 And let me warm you when cold?

Is my fire too hot?
 Is my spirit too bold?

Will you be at the tree?
 When it's all over and told?

I love you so much, and I hope you can see.
 You've opened my eyes, and now I can see.

   In every breath I take, I ask for your air.

   While I tease my emotions, I don't even care.

You tease me too, and I probably let you,
            That is because I just can't forget you.

You fill my minutes with sixty even seconds,
          Your love is my compass, in every direction.

 I want to find you, but you always hide.

                Hide and seek....

        Conquer ...

   And divide.

From Ryan McJury

The world is my love,

  Impressed by her splendor.

If love was for sale,

  There would be a love vendor.

And visit he or she and you'd find,

  That love could be bought, all of the time.

But that is a place that will never exist,

  Love can't be bought. There's no price on a kiss.

Thank god for love and for those who find it.

  Love is not for sale, and you can't rewind it.

If love is gone, can you find it again?

  If you're alone, will the loneliness end?

My advice to you

Sever your ties to a cause so obviously evil.

Devote your life to all other people.

Exhaust a moment, and then begin another.

Nothing can soothe you, just like each other.

Grow in peace, or grow in violence,

Love and war, then death and silence.

A Great Poem

Worth of what where?
  I really don't care.

  If I could put it more clearly,
                      I would.

The pain in my head,
              Is too greater dead,

  In life there's more evil than good? No.

    Fist full of dollars,

                  And a head full of holes.

  Swiss cheese holes in my head!

  What's the time?

             Where am I?

                    And, am I already dead?

Shoot at the night,

                    To cast out the light,

And bring out the moon, to boot.

Each word is a fire, each letter a spark,

There was only one of me on Noah's Ark.

First you must see, and then you can look,

  Uncover the meaning inside this book.

In time translated …

        Circumnavigated …
                Enlightened …
                      Awakened …

        Emancipated.

Untitled

The mysteries of life aren't mysteries at all.

  If you look, listen, and feel,

Then you can solve them all.

  Solve them not with answers,

But, with your own good intuition.

  Since the day that you were born,

You've been on a mission.

  The mission is to seek,

So seek and you shall find.

  All the answers in life are out there,

And all are intertwined.

  As you follow the path …

And move on down the line …

  Any direction that you go …

Be sure to stop …

  And read the sign.

Untitled

Writing and still sighting,

    Thoughts constantly igniting.

At a thousand R.P.M.'s,

    My mind is de-lighting.

And most of it, it seems,

    Is not reality, but dreams,

Since the world we've created,

    Is faulting at the seams.

Then the light, it came in.

    To some it brought them in.

But to others, who just watched,

    It was like the time that's on a clock.

So we sat, and we looked.

    We waited once again.

For the right time to tell you,

    About the fables they defend.

And in time and in space,

    All the answers are erased,

The only thing that we know,

Is that we come from outer space!

Time is the same as emptiness

Most of what I write can fit on one page.

The time and the place are older than age.

But so deep it is,

    You must not dig it with a shovel.

For what you are digging for,

    May bring you trouble.

Time on the double,

    And sped up by others,

The life that we live,

    Is a gift from our mother.

And too often we find,

    The bounds are defined.

If you incline to me,

    You may be declined.

But some, who can see it,

    Don't know how to look.

The map and the legend,

    Are revealed inside this book.

As you receive the message

As a person, you are a microphone,

    You pick up on subtle sounds.

Don't look first,

    Just jump feet first,

You too can exceed the bounds.

    A second is an hour,

And an hour is a minute.

    There is no beginning,

Everything is infinite!

    Now we're getting somewhere,

And I hope it's where we're going.

    If you can't understand it,

Then its time you started knowing.

    Come on in the door is open.

You don't need a key.

    Know that you know nothing,

And to see it, you must be.

But what you are looking for, you can't always feel,

Just because you can touch it, does not mean it's real.

Untitled

It's not so simple or plain,
To sit and watch it rain,

Water falling from the sky,
Is kind of weird and strange.

And my life is the same.
It's not so simple or plain.

I see things a little different.
So, to some, I'm weird and strange.

But it is clear to me …
That to be, you must be.

The meaning of all life,
Is so clear to see.

To love, and to live,
And not to get, but to give.

Be kind to one another,
And let your heart forgive.

It's simple, it sounds.
But it is all around.

So you filter out the bad,
Inch for inch, and pound for pound.

It is far, and it is near,
I have lost all my fear,

The things I know now,
Could not be more clear.

It's a picture …
Painted by calamity …

A surreal image hung,
In the hall of humanity.

You see it everyday,
And it has an evil way,

To make it not look bad,
People give it away.

It is totally wrong,
And you are totally right,

Some call it noon,
Others call it midnight.

I find that I try.
And I find that I don't.

So I write it all down,
Or maybe I won't.

I'll do all that I can,
But I can never do it all.

It can be very big,
And it can also be small.

Do you know what it is?
Maybe you can know it.

Just because you reaped it,
Does it mean you sowed it?

Nothing

Twenty three is a number …
That stands next to twenty four.

Twenty five is a number,
That can unlock the final door.

Sixty seven and fifty two,
And forty three ten thousand million.

Are the numbers I express …
To the one in the one trillion.

Eighty five and twenty two,
Are equal the way I see it.

Thirty six and fifty four,
Are the numbers, you can be it.

"What is it", you ask.
And was I even told?

I learned you are number …
You are so young, and yet so old.

As I travel through the spaces,
And I travel through the times.

I am the one to reveal …
That In life, you often find.

That, are we us?
And who are they,

No fast forward?
And no rewind?

Though I teach the lesson,
I am a student lost in time.

See the point

Life, love, and death, and a constant pain,
  Are as sure as the sun, the sky, and the rain.

So sure, that they are not taken ever so lightly.
  I felt unsure once, but just ever so slightly.

Have you ever asked a question,
  And the answer was the same?

Have you ever seen a fire,
  That did not have a flame?

And did you ever meet a person,
  But did not get their name?

And in the end you'll find,
  That it is all the same.

There was never such a person,
  There was never such a name.

So you patch a hole,
  In the hull of time …

So the space won't exceed,
  The bounds, that are defined.

I Live on the top of the highest peak.
  Olympus Mons, The side Oblique.

So society's children are scared into reason.
  Spreading a lie, is a true act of treason.

A flower to bloom,
  In the footprints of space.

Then the custom of the sea,
  Was set into place.

A number is a letter

One is not two, and two is not three,
  But four is all of five.
Six is not seven, but seven is eight,
  And nine is not alive!

You never mind the banter,
  You're confused, and misled.
If you don't wave a banner,
  Why do you burn one instead?

Modify your thinking,
  Into seeing what is there,
Look at the Chessboard,
  And move, if you dare.

Converting all their principles,
  Into laws and actions,
Kind of like a math problem,
  With decimals and fractions.

I felt it, so I thought it.
  Now to me it's all the same.
Their business is a monopoly.
  It's nothing but a game.

A game you play, it is made up,
  And so is so called "Time".

I live in singularity,

    In a black hole,

        In my mind.

A letter is a number

Deactivate your senses,

    And listen to good reason.

        Just because you're hunting,

    Does not mean its season.

List of laws, with knicks and flaws,

    I'm seeing through the shadows.

I know, I feel.

    I lost a great deal.

        Silently screaming, like tomatoes.

        Cut and scared, diced and marred,

I'm a little bit off kilter,

    Just like your lung, and also your eyes,

        Your craniobulum is a filter.

So I sift, and I drift,

    I'm awake when I fly.

    I'll fly any other spaceship.

A voyage I do take, and a course I do see.

    I'm a hurricane and an earthquake!

A Question

Evidently you are amazing,
 And yet virtually impossible.
But somehow you exist,
 However apparently implausible.

So sublime, and esoteric
 Eminently Inconsistent
Celebrate the celebration
 Just in time to miss it.

Many years of tears and fears,
 And the end of the individual.
Compressed, condensed, confused,
 Removed, the damage is residual.

No more old ways …
  Or useless days …
    Clammering up the masses.

Stifled and stammered,
  Congruently hammered.

The threat has been there always.

So they sit in the dark,
 And they lie in the day,
An eagle has great vision.

You run like a rat,
  You hide under a rock,
    Your freedom is your prison.

Scissors cut through paper,
 And paper covers rock.
 Rock smashes scissors,
  But what can stop the clock?

Ry an McJu Ry

The first two are the last two.

It's not just an illusion.

There's no third one,

Or no fourth one.

    Let's end all this confusion.

And I told you, when you found the hidden messages,

It's in everything you write,

And you didn't get my message.

Still waiting …

Still waiting for who?

And once you understand,

You'll know part one,

And then part two.

Untitled

If you saw it, would you know it?

  If you knew it, could you see?

Every question has an answer,

  You pay the price, it isn't free.

And what's the cost per hour?

  Could you break it down to minutes?

But a second is an hour,

  And everything is infinite.

To love, you must pay?

  Money, time, attention, and affection?

And what do you receive in return?

  Don't ask me, I don't know.

    I paid, and I got burned.

What do you call it

Ordinary looking,
    But special deep inside.

Once you find it,
    You will know it.

There's no question,
    You can't hide.

Then you'll show it,
But not on purpose,

People will just feel it.

… It could be strong.
It could be subtle.

… It is the "Holy Spirit."

The "Holiest of the Holies",
Is somewhere deep within.

Search and you will see.
Just be, and you will be.

There is no prerequisite,
And the cost is free.

But, there is a price,
And steep it is,

You pay it with your life.

Some pay more …

    Some pay less …

        Some feel pleasure,

Some feel strife.

What could be

I looked and I saw nothing.

I looked again and saw the same.

Then I looked a third time,

And found out it was a game.

What are the odds to win?

And in the end, is there a winner?

Some will win, some will lose.

If you lose, are you a sinner?

You played the game, and you lost,

Took the test, and you did fail.

Wait your turn to try again,

This time don't turn tail.

32

The two crosses …

Move slowly in the sky.

Merging toward the center to form the eight spoked wheel of time.

The state of being is all one existence.

You are because you are.

What you call "God" is the state of being itself.

As the creator creates the created,

The created create the creator.

And the created create new life themselves.

Which came first?

The creator, or the created?

Or, are they one in the same?

It is all related.

All relative.

The only thing that actually is …

Is being itself.

Everything else is NOT.

All conditions of being, all phenomena, exist simultaneously,

Occupying the same space at the same time.

Time is not real. It is only relative.

And the wheels on the Buddha's feet contain the thirty two spokes.

The path has eight petals. The flower is eight fold.

The Poet

Ordinary original optimism.

Alliterating while aggregated.

Spread the word, free the bird.

Their method is overrated.

Follow all their leads.

Do all their bad deeds.

But what are you left with?

And does it meet your needs?

Sort of round,

I'm out of bounds.

Do I measure up?

Who did you think I'd be?

I told you I'd grow up!

34

An eyebrow raises to the insignificant wind from afar.

A man stood in awe …

Others lost all sanity …

Women and children cry …

Insignificance, no longer.

A family of silence echoes.

Their cries are heard.

When will they ask for my definition?

Who will ask?

A rock lays undisturbed …

Silent …

Peaceful …

But, when the wrong animal comes along to move that rock,

Or stack it upon another …

It is no longer undisturbed …

Nor peaceful.

The Bet

A fortress of wounds,

    Held together by sadness,

Is the beat of a drum,

    And the rhythm of madness.

Some cry until tears fill up their eyes,

They hurt … They are in pain,

    And then they realize.

They are the holders of life,

    And they remain strong,

As the future for all,

    Plays out in a song.

That song was written many years ago,

And you know all the words …

    … Just so you know.

We Win

Life, love, and death,

    And a constant pain.

Are as sure as the sun,

    The sky,

        And the rain.

So sure,

    That they are not taken ever so lightly,

I feel the good winning,

    But just ever so slightly.

The Tree

Lonely, I sat hastened by life.

  One minute, one second.

        It was all strife.

Pain and suffering,

    I had known way to well,

I prayed for a heaven,
        Because was my life hell?

If I fell, straight from the sky,

  Then where is my home?

      And, why can't I fly?

So high, that I wish I was higher,

    So I awake through meditation,

  And see the truth is on fire.

Of Life

A flower is an etching,

In the cornerstone of time.

A lemon is just a

Yellow version of a lime.

In time we'll find,

That it will probably be,

The meaning of all life,

Is found inside a tree.

Summertime

In a time of silence,

In a sea of beauty.

Your eyes glance,

You see right through me.

I can see you,

Do you want me to look?

If I opened the cover,

Would you read the book?

Love

Two butterflies play in the breeze.

Chasing and following,

        Then hiding and seeking.

To be so free as to fly,

      So, I reply

"What a Beautiful world to see!"

"You can't deny."

Floating and fluttering,

    Two butterflies buttering.

So simple to love,

      Uncover the covering.

          Two butterflies fly.

An equation

Since I have a lot of love to give,

    Since I have a strong will to live.

Though I hope we multiply,

    I must first … tell you why …

Divide or add,

    And then subtract,

I'm sure I'd want to then come back.

    Evolve, evade, in time to see,

        The answer is not always three.

Expect, deplore,

    Declare, decry.

        I wish that you … could learn to fly.

And not to look as an observer,

    Not just any time conserver.

Waste all time,

    Nickel … Dime …

        Infinity is too sublime!

Is the answer to your question

Gorge of insane distances,

The Canyon of the Moon,

Just inside the doorway,

Is the one you call "Hatu".

He will take you up the staircase,

And lead you to the portal.

In the Mountains of Moriah,

Just west of the border.

Living the legend,

In the mountain, you will find,

That reality is just a dream,

In someone else's mind.

I am

A treetop is my steeple,
   So I hear all of the forest,

The more I grow,
   The rest I show,
      That's why I'm not the poorest.

Rich in green with lavish leaves,
   And lush alliteration.

Christian, Muslim, and Jew,
   Under God we're all one nation?

I see a thought,
   I grab a thought to expand upon my knowledge.

I've got to go express myself …
      But expression has been abolished.
I ask of you, if you can see,
      Or are you blind and out of feeling?

Just drop a line, and hook a fish,
      And then continue reeling.

Did you catch a sea creature?
         Or did you catch yourself?

Could you tell that it was you?
            Are you a hazard to your health?

Who

        I'm not tragic

                I'm tried and trued

    I'm not stupid

            I'm slightly clued

You think I'm crazy

            And my view is askew

    Why can't we live in peace

              Is my message to you

The Old Dog

To believe in nature's prowess,
A population had to ask.
If any was a lesson,
If all effort was a task.

I expand upon the dream of freedom,
From the ever oppressive system.
So many a law has been broke,
I cannot begin to list 'em.

An old dog was lay to rest,
In a manner of no reverence.
His service to his country was life.
And the fight for freedom caused this severance.

The old dog was an American long forgotten …
Who hadn't lost faith, in the world's most feared decision.

Exist in war, or die for peace?
Was the old dog's last commission.

To evaluate the flooded sea,
So full and yet so fragile!

I ask of you,

        Just for once.

    Just pay, and do not haggle.

Never quits

In every time of relative importance,
There comes a choice of time, speed, or distance.

To exist in life, on this level of significance,
Is often seen as resistance.

Sell your idea for a dollar or a yen,
    Make another dollar,
        Then buy it back again.

America! America!
In these United States.

One hundred million thousand,
Twisted dreams and fates.

Serve your inner selfishness,
And often times you'll see,

You probably should not have done that, gee.

Order from an order form,
And talk into the speaker.

Look into the camera,
Do you feel any weaker?

Don't feel weak,
Be strong and speak!

Then the words have all been told,
Much more wealth,

That can be found,
Than in a pot of gold!

Really

Resolve to amuse yourself,

    And slowly place the instrument of delusion,

        Amongst your most vital vitality.

Obviously you seem to recognize the signs.

Your path is one not condemned.

You seek answers,

    Answers I have.

        But are your questions true?

Do you need a demonstration?

A light show perhaps?

    A miracle from a divine presence?

        …. Relapse.

No important association with an actual factual fact!

"I paid the fee, I did not see, I want my money back!"

A tic, a tac, a toe …

    And though, it may have platinum colored label …

    Often times the truth is nothing but a fable!

Where

Do you know who I am?

Do you know where I go?

Do you see what I see?

Do you know what I know?

Am I a "Ryan", or a "McJury"?

Or a version of something new?

I am only one of many,

To enlighten your new view.

We see it now together …

    And only time will tell,

        You will live my visions,

And all is not quite well.

First you must test,

    And then you can rest.

The finding of secrets …

        Is no easy test.

To test or be tested,

    Then simply be bested,

        By virtue of freedom,

    Cannot be contested.

The

Look out the window as life passes by.

Inside do you fear that the pain will reside?

A tree will stand tall,

    And survive for all existence.

But could you withstand the threat of persistence?

Delusions and myths,

    Convincing to some.

Was the last of all war,

    And then there was none.

What

Except in time,

We are sublime.

I've crossed the fourth dimensions lines.

Time and space,

The speed of light.

Magnified by one million times,

But is it right?

Day, or night,

I ask the question:

Am I in ... the fifth dimension?

Lunacy Up There

Why do you torment me … Moon?
        What are you looking at … Moon?

I wonder how many people are looking at you,
        Asking you why you torment them …

        … Too?

            …. Moon!

I look at you.
        You look at me me.

        Me.…   You.…

            I.…
        Moon!

Many an infinite soul,
        Have stared at you cold.

Yet, you still stare back,
        You are older than old.

Each of our long stares,
          Is just a split second of your existence.

Some gather in your light,
      To fight,
           For what is right,
               Through pain and persistence.

Others see love lost … remembering a time,

When the one you love pointed at the moon,
    And said "Kiss me."

Except I still love her,
    And she does not love me.

Every time I look at you moon,
    My heart hurts.

    I'm sad and lonely,
         Just like you moon.

Where

Bad dreams,
    Fields and streams,

I'm living in the forest.

I Look,
    I Love …

You'd think I was the poorest.

I think,
    I blink,
Only once for good measure,

I paced, I dug,
    I found the buried treasure.

A map,
    I read it,

I looked at the legend.

Decoded, Deciphered.

There are two ones in eleven.

At night

Repeat it twice.

    Three times is thrice.

Who should you be on Halloween?

Or, maybe you already are …

    A prime example of mean …

Scary and such …

    Too scared, too much …

Wake up at night in cold sweats?

    Hot flashes it seems,

        I die in my dreams.

Every night for me is Halloween.

There is a light

A riddle

    Is a puzzle

        Its pieces in your mind

A drop is a puddle

    It's a river

        For all time

A look

    Is a feeling

    It's an example

  For our kind

A thought is a theory

It's a threat to their find

Adrift

"They're not ever understanding."

"The voice is so commanding."

"Go to the water",

    "Don't be so demanding."

Needless to say …
    But simple to imply …

Just because you are a bird,
    Does not mean that you can fly.

"Open up the puzzle."
    "Piece it all together."

"Tear down the castles."
    "End the stormy weather"

"Negotiate with your opponent."
    "No, I think that you shouldn't."

Should you go quietly, like they say?

    There's no way. You just shouldn't!

On the island

Never ending,
    Ongoing and bending.

Twisting, refracting,
    A message I'm sending.

I'm lending.
    You're receiving.

Don't forget to give back.

But don't give back to me.

NOTHING IS A FACT.

Give to another,
    Now do you see the circle?

It's a process that progresses.

Blue and red equals purple.

But what is green and orange?

And is red a fire?

I escaped from my illusions,
    And was burned up in a pyre.

I followed a trail back to life,
    And I emerged from my cocoon.

You must leave everything behind,
    When you are standing on the moon.

You can

I lived and then I died,
   The whole time I was alive.
I thought it, then I saw it,
   And I flew straight through the sky.
I needed nothing to survive,
   Except for rational thoughts.
Thinking and predicting,
   But there's one thing that I sought.
You may know what it was,
   You may know what it is not.
Because I seek one thing,
   Can you see it up above?
      Did I find it?
         Or lose it?
            Or give it to you?
               … Love

Find truth

I feel as though I look through a world that's left unseen.

I see through the shadows,

    And the wavelengths in between.

A spectrum,

    Roy G. Biv

        But what else could there be?

One million thousand colors are visible to me.

    Can you see them?

        Do you look?

            Or are you to blind to perceive?

It's time you started listening,

    And starting to believe.

Look upon the legend.

    A flower is a signal.

        The sun is just a battery,

        And we are the original!

Universal Things

Defending and bending.
    The messages I'm sending.

It's all ending,
    Quit befriending.
The evil is intending.

You can see it, but you can't.
    Its frequency is hidden.

A wavelength that's left out,
    In the codes that you were given.

A fortress is an ocean,
    And the beaches are its walls.

If justice permits,
    Then liberty won't fall!

Install and override,
    Download into memory.

A sequence in life,
    Is just a page in a story.

Addition and subtraction,
    But to me they're both the same.

You're nothing but a ball inside a pinball game.

Fate is the flipper.

    You're on a trip, so you're a tripper.

And you are bouncing around under glass!

    As the forces have predicted.

        Then the good will win, at last.

Reveal the lie

They composed a set of words,
And say, "Because it's so!"

I don't believe any of it,
Just so you know.

You're falling for a trick,
A prank if you will,

The joke is reality,
Nothing is not nil.

Your mind is a prison,
If you let it lock you in.

Or, you can have it opened,
By awakening within.

Overcome the obstacles,
See through the lies.

Are we all blind sheep?
In other being's eyes.

They're commanding laws, as I'm exposing flaws,
In their little scheme,
I'm negotiating,
They're captivating,
It's not easy being green.

Not The Wizard of Oz

Pray tell!

    Do you know?

Who is behind the curtain?

It's not the Wizard of Oz,

    But, who can be certain?

Does he cast a shadow?

    As he presses the buttons,

And does he know the time?

    Is it now, all of a sudden?

We look, but do we see?

    You are the same as me.

    For some who have found it,

    The answer is to be.

So select and so few,

    That I need to set it right....

The eightfold path, to encompass the light!

Avolokiteshvara

Is life combined with existence in time?
      And just who's on your side, do you know?
The closer we get, the further we are,
    And the outside is just for show.
But go deep inside,
    In the mind's divide,
And you'll continue to grow.
    Empty in time,
        Compassion combined,
Then you will emit a rare glow.
    Vibrations and light, providing delight,
        To all those who you encounter.
A stream you have entered,
    A stream you have crossed,
        There is no point here to be countered.
So simple it sounds,
    That a sphere is still round,
        But a cube is no longer a square!
As theories are tested,
    The good are contested.
        It's time to speak up, do you dare?
Although it's not real,
    All that you feel,
        You're emotions are only a cage.

Open the lock, then look at the clock,
          No number can measure your age.
                    Time is on the double.
Are we in trouble?
          But just who is a never returner?
                Nirvana it seems, I saw in dream,
But, I too am just a learner.
        The fabric of time …
              Suspenseful …
                  Sublime …
I think I know the secret.
          Time is not real.
              What you see, you can't fear.
    If you sow it, then you can reap it.
A steady wave upon the sea, is a sign that we are free.
Example of sounds, my thoughts have no bounds,
      And no one's more sure than me,

  All conditions of being exist,
        Occupying the same space,

    SI—MUL—TAN—E—OUS—LY

Light Bright

Wheel of time revolving.
    Clouds of dust evolving.

Mysteries elude,
    Conclusions conclude,
        But some problems still need solving.

Answers are few,
    And theories are vast.

None of our future we'll learn from the past.

And so on, and so on, until repeated …

The Sun and the Moon,
    The Earth and its sea,
        Good can never be defeated!

    Six equals seven,
        And five equals four.

    I stand on the ceiling,
        And look at the floor.

    Sideways, it seems …
        I fly in my dreams,
            The colors of red are blue.

        And who's in our head?
I'm alive while I'm dead.
And who is more me than you?

Tractor

Loose bolts on a tractor,
   I fly in on beams of light.

I open up the clouds,
   And then I take my flight.

I soar through dimensions,
   And often times I see,

That I always miss that tractor,
   And think it misses me.

It clanks like my brain does,
   As I mosey down the road.

My spaceship is no Cadillac,
   It's a tractor, pulling a load.

I understand the notion,
   That we exist on several planes …

As we motion through the universe,
   In the high speed traffic lanes.

Passing all the tourist traps,
   As we approach the original source.

The stars are just a roadmap,
   And we are on the course.

Of Infinology

Always loving,

    Never needing …

If you asked me "Was I speeding?"

I'd say, "No sir I was not,

    Yet, I am constantly exceeding."

"Was I exceeding?"

    I'd say, "No sir."

    "How could I promulgate the future?"

I'd say, "Look over there!

    It's the path that will suit you."

"But the path over yonder,

    Is a dark one filled with visions,

And your mind is the path,

That can free you from division."

And division is a process, not understood by many,

I looked inside one number, and saw that it was plenty.

DECODES THE FINAL MESSAGE

Thoughts manifest,
As I digress.

I see through the lies,
And I'll finish the test.

I'll pass, and then to where?
Do you know just where you're going?

If you're looking for the answers …
What is it that you are knowing?

If you grew into pure space …
And ended in white light …

The sun goes down,
The moon comes up,

And then we call it night?

And we are

A peaceful tree,
  A summer night,
    And a winter sun in rain …

A mountain in a waterfall,
    Is a sight I've seen explained.

But a Ferris wheel,
      A Universe,
         And the time that's on a clock …

A calendar,
    A zodiac,
        And the being you unlock.

Sight the presence,
        See the tree!

The tree is not made of rock.

A time to be there,
    And where is there?

And who else are you really?

You were never there,
    You're not there now,
        And you never will be …

            Really.

Renters

How can land be sold?

You really cannot own it.

Expanding in my heart, is love …

And that is why I've shown it.

I see the love,

I feel the love,

And that is why I've sent it,

I command the good to inhabit this world,

And the evil must now exit.

In life you really cannot own a thing,

So that is why you rent it.

For Laura Lynn

Love at first sight,

    I thought was not true.

And that is what I thought,

    Until, I met you.

Your smile and grace,

    And beauty, overpowering.

I exploded with love,

    Like a meteor, showering.

I looked in your eyes,

    And our souls joined together.

And then when we spoke,

    It was like I'd known you forever,

I wish I could tell you,

Just what will come next.

But that's up to fate …

    And I'm out of context.

Soul Tape

If tape could hold together love,

There would be a great demand for tape.

Would it hold forever?

What bonds souls?

Is it soul tape?

Where can I get soul tape?

I love her.

She does not love me anymore.

I wonder if it is too late for soul tape.

I don't think she remembers me.

Sound of space

Nothing is sound.

A thought is around.

Will anyone break the circle?

Over it unders,

And sideways it seems,

The color of red is purple.

A flower is lost.

But what is the cost?

And little it seems can be done.

So listen and feel,

Scorched a great deal,

Icarus flew too close to the sun.

Nothing is some, and something is none.

Who is keeping the score?

Fighting each other, like animals in packs.

It was who, who started this war?

Mirrors in time

I'm living, and still breathing.

I'M NOT SURE IF I'M BELIEVING.

I feel that I've been tricked,

And that life is so deceiving.

I looked upon a scene,

I saw the king and queen.

I understood the messages,

Two aces, eights in between.

A sorrow filled delight,

Is a summer wind in rain.

Complicated … Coordinated …

But to some, I am quite plain.

Ordinary looking …

So that one must look within.

There's never a time I frown,

So frequently, I grin.

A look from deep within,

Will save you from your sorrow,

I share it with the world,

So you never have to borrow.

Forever
For Laura Lynn

If you need a crutch,

Prop yourself up on my shoulder.

I will hold you up and love you,

Until we are both unable to stand together.

Then together, we will fall to a place

That we are both unfamiliar with,

Yet know so well.

We have seen it in our dreams.

The rain is not cold or wet.

The sun is not hot, or too bright,

A cool breeze, prevails.

A bird's song so sweet …

                So infinite …

        Perfect.

Perfect, like you.

Perfect to me.

Love would survive …

Forever.

Love will survive …
                Our love …

        Forever.

Forever 2
For Laura Lynn

Please hear my love,

And return my call.

I love you, I do.

The amount is not small.

All the wishes, I've wished,

Were only for you ...

For you to be happy,

And that to be true.

I can't explain how,

And I can't explain why,

But I miss you so much,

That I often cry.

This may go on,

Until the day, that I die.

The impression you made,

Was love, and so pure.

I'll love you forever,

    And that,

        I am sure.

Forever 3
For Laura Lynn

As I sit in solitude,
I ponder my brainwaves.

They are simple to define,
But are too indecipherable.

She is my love.
And, I am her nothing.

I wonder if she remembers me,
Often, throughout the day.

A ghost of a love, long gone away.

Sometimes when I awake,
She is kissing me, in my dreams.

Will this go on forever, I ask?

Possibly broken,
My brain still sends me signals.

Signals of her soft lips,
Kissing me in the night.

A slow dance to be stepped to,
In the middle of city streets.

Her eyes filled with understanding for me,
And I hers,

For all eternity.
Forever.

Untitled

A space filled with darkness,

Is full of emptiness.

As the darkness formulates its plan,

It slowly emerges from the space.

Then the light comes in.

"Light meets darkness. Are they are one in the same?"

"They are, and are not."

As the existence persists in space.

The Demon

Go to the keeper of the night,

And ask for a gift in the form of personal satisfaction.

Then your soul is not yours any longer, and you lost!

Light the fire of never ending evil,

And despair flows steadily through your veins,

Overpowering the naturally instilled traits …

Set into motion by consumption.

Who knew you would go to the level of the insects,

That thrive off the crumbs of the general population.

Dead and walking.

"Undo this!" you plead.

He hears you …

Then laughs …

Only to find,

You both benefited.

Unable to control the functions of your fate,

After life passes through your soul's chariot.

Nothing can save you, and your path is etched in the slate of time.

And that, is an unfortunate journey to embark upon.

Peace be with you.

Silence is calling

Answer your phone.
Is it him on the line?

"I'll just be one second,
Is one second fine?"

"One second is fine",
Is what you might say …

Or you may hang up,
And spare no delay.

It doesn't matter,
There's nothing you can do.

His name is a mystery …
And he's come for you.

Epitaph

I opened up a door,
And inside sat death.

As I walked in,
I drew my last breath.

He greeted me kindly,
Like I was no stranger.

When I stepped forward,
I knew no danger.

It didn't matter,
I couldn't tempt fate.

As time increased,
I felt I was late.

Later or earlier,
I was deceased.

And at long last,
I received inner peace.

Nirvana

Growing, and knowing,
I AM NOT THE FIRST.

I began to grow more,
As I stepped on the Earth.

Still growing, I grew.
I was walking on stars.

They grew smaller, I grew larger
Then larger, and large.

Walking on solar systems,
Still growing bigger,

The Universe became small,
Too small to figure.

Then I grew out of the cosmos,
Into clear white empty space.

Then I knew that I had arrived,
In my final resting place.

The End

The time and the place,
    Is always changing.

Nothing is constant,
    Re-arranging.

Seeing the true entity,
    Looking between the known.

Exemplifying the Buddha,
    Outside of the koan.

A planet is an island,
    And so near is its shore,

To some it is a ceiling,
    To others it's a floor.

My point exactly is …
    That they're never really is one.

So many beings look at it,
    But to us, it's just our sun.

If I asked the universe,
    What's in twenty twelve?

The universe would answer,
    "On earth, you call it hell!"

Earth quaking, and shaking,
    And seas overflowing,

The Maya, I Ching …
    All of them knowing.

Others would guess,
    How could it be?

Every so often,
    We go into the sea.

What can be done?
    The poles, they may shift.

And then there was none,
    From a wave that's so swift.

A black hole at its center,
    In life, you're a renter.

The universe is constant,
    As the singularity, you enter.

No time, or space,
    Just where is this place?

Gravity pulling,
    At a very fast pace,

For some years we've known,
    It can't be erased.

A mind is a star,
    And a star is just dust,

Please understand,
    You are metal, you rust!

So, we will see,
    We might have to see.

What just will happen,
    And just what will be.

Nothing can save you,
    Not even your fate.

I knew it would happen,
    Better sooner, than late.

Out of the greatest evil,
    Will come the greatest good.

The sun will lead us,
    To just where it should.

Some will survive,
    Some will just know,

Some will just not,
    And some will just go.

The ocean is a world,
    We come from its heart.

A single cell existed,
    And that was the start.

Kalpa after kalpa,
    Time after time,

I understand the message,
    And how it's defined.

The signals are out there,
    And now all are aligned.

Many have a theory,
    So few have a thought,

Existing in a world surreal,
    Your freedom can't be bought!

A single understanding,
    A single place in time,

I looked inside the future,
    And saw the vast sublime.

Yet the past has been lost.
    They burned most of the records,

Except for the Akashic,
    Around it, we are centered.

Others are out there,
    You can see them in your mind.

I looked through a prism,
    And just what did I find?

I found under a microscope,
    We are infinitely small.

Where is here, just what is clear?
    And what can you recall?

A sum is a total,
    A formula for math,

A can is a storage unit,
    Where you put your trash.

Take waste and trash, and dump them out,
    A planet is polluted in a flash.

Polluted and disposed,
    It is garbage we compose.

There may be a time; there may be a place
    Is it you, that is understanding?

And who can clean the Earth,
    Of the garbage that is expanding?

You can clean it.
    You can fix it.

We all must do our part.
    Those who pollute, those who waste …

Must be shown the heart,
    The heart is the center.

The center of your being.

Look out the window.
    What do you see?

Is it you, that you are seeing?

Sun is shining, and the breezes are blowing …

    I'm sending the teaching,
        Yet, so few are knowing.

Who Am I

I'm yelling….

Can you hear me?

I'm Knocking on your cranium!

Some say I'm Eighty-eight,
The atomic number of the Radium.

I've never been uranium,
Though I am atomic.

Smaller than a particle,
You could say that I'm ion-ic.

There are as many constellations,
And keys on the piano.

I'm sending you a signal,
Can you understand, though?

A frequency …

A channel …

Can you tune it in?

What is the purpose?

Will you lose, or can you win?

I'm Mercury's year,
     My thoughts are so clear.

What is it you call "the being"?

After Two hundred eighty million years I've found,

The question is worth revealing.

I want to go home,
Maybe this time,

If I illuminate your path.

The answer is a problem,
That you cannot solve with math.

Solve it with the truth,
A myth is a lie,

But many believe it is true.

Look inside yourself,
You yourself are the only clue.

It's blue,
It's red,
It's yellow.

All of them are primary.

Though there are the three,
Two of them are binary.

Complex, because you make it,
Simple if you listen.

You too can hear it,
And help me on my mission.

Spread peace and love.
Look up above.

Understanding is the secret.

Just because you've seen the light,
Does not mean that you've received it.

Does it matter

It doesn't matter who you are.

It doesn't matter where you go.

You are here, and there.

Is all you really need to know.

It doesn't matter where you are.

It doesn't matter what you know.

You are you, and that is that.

And the answer is … to grow.

To grow to where, to do what?

And who is the super being?

Look in the mirror …

Is it me?

Or is it you …

That you are seeing!

Don't misunderstand,

According to the plan,

Looking in the mirror, you can see us …

If you can.

88

The sun will shine bright.
A breeze will blow cool.

The love will spread out.
I am no fool.

I mean it,
I'll prove it.

We all will find peace.

I'll show it,
You'll see it.

The war will then cease.

A bird will fly far,
And a fish will swim near me.

As I am swimming,
The darkness will fear me.

Swimming in galaxies …
… The universe wide.

As I call out …
… The destructive will hide.

Being and living are so very opposite.

You must make them one,
And then never stop with it!

Where

A gift of love,

Was thrown into a fire.

It exploded,

Then, spilled out all my desire.

A soft spoken word,

That would sound so loving …

A the band played louder,

The fans kept on shoving.

As they moshed, and they pitted.

Not a one benefited.

What you want to understand,

Can now be permitted.

In the house

A Glorious fire,

Set by a notorious love.

Was the gift of an angel,

From so far above.

She hits me with sweetness,

And makes me feel wanted.

Her love is my house,

And my house is haunted.

It's not me

Some healthy are sick,
And some sick are fine.
Do you know who I am?
Just look at the time.

It's not hard to figure,
I've been around a while.
You know in your heart …
I'm who makes you smile.

And sometimes, you cry,
Or get sad and down.
And that's also me.
I'm who makes you frown.

But the one who makes you rage …
And boil with anger …
Is the one to look out for …
He's nothing but DANGER.

Behind the curtain

I'm on my way,
Can you see me?

I'm almost surely there.

I need to see something.
So find me, if you dare.

A tee vee set, a radio,
And a satellite you say …

A spaceship, and a tractor beam,
Are my mode of choice today.

I will arrive …
Then I will ask …
As my pen could surely tell you …

Who is who,
And where are you …
What else can they sell you?

Nothing more, nothing less …
The truth is truly free.

Nothing less, and nothing more …
The truth is surely me.

I'm on my way …
    I'm not a hoax.

I won't promise it will be easy.
    It's not so hard to find me …

If you are seeing, then you can be me.
Yes you are.
A planet,
A star,
An interstellar being.

Look at me.
What do you see?
It's you, that you are seeing.

Coordinate

Resolve the resolutions,
Or continue to dissolve.
I'm confused with illusions.
It's a problem to be solved.

So I decipher the illustration,
Of what we call reality.
A portrait of time,
In the hall of humanity.

Everyday you are tricked,
And you don't even know.
You think that you are free …
But where else can you go?

To know what I know,
Is to know some things are false.
Some energy has been taken.
And hidden behind walls.

Except you don't even know it,
It's kind of like a fraction
You are the numerator and denominator
The division is distraction.

Many things are false.
Not all what we see is true, except a source,
Or sources somewhere,
Are related to me and you.

That is all that ever happened.
The prophets are just masters.
Enlightened to the truth,
To warn you of disasters.

Disasters of illusions,
And distortion of their teaching.
Awaken and you'll see,
That we all are still seeking.

Seeking the final truth,
Seeking the final being,
Seeking the ultimate knowledge,
That has been so deceiving.

You are the force itself,
It can be good, and also evil.
You are the one to answer to,
You are one with all the people.

I'm sure that this is true.
I've researched all the evidence,
From another time and place,
Our ancestors made their residence.

And the stars, and the sky …
Are their congress and president.
However there is source …
And its force is so evident.

The teller of tales

Negotiate with the illusion?
No, I don't think that I will.

I don't find it necessary,
To entertain, or thrill.

We must get back, what we lack,
Or get lost in the commotion.

Second you have a thought,
But first you have a notion.

Anytime I listen,
And anytime I feel,
I look into the air,
If you see it, is it real?

A green state of loving,
   Lavish with tranquility,
A low loving motion …
   Impressed by her ability.

A seed to plant,
   Is a flower in her forest.
A look is love,
   We push and shove …
     We are the richest, yet the poorest?

I need to see, just let me be.
   I'm doing all I can.
     Relentlessly I do my task,
       According to the plan.

A plan is a vision …
And a vision is a dream.

But a dream is fact, nor fiction.
Until I intervene!

Explain to who, and are you sure?
Who told you that it's so?

Apologize, no I despise.
Why won't they let you know?

I saw a piece of life.
A puzzle, if you will …

Negotiate, interpolate!
Why does your God kill?

Mine does not … I have a thought.
A notion if you please:

I looked,
    I leapt,
        I flew,
            I fell,
And landed in a tree.

I broke a branch,
I hit my head,
And suffered a fatal shock …

There is no such thing as time,
        Or the numbers on a clock.

Untitled

Confused, but committed.
The truth has been omitted,
And what we think we know,
Is what we've been bullshitted.

I dare to ask the questions,
That don't have any answers.
The stars move through the night,
Like a million little dancers.

I fortify my presence,
With accents of projection.
I send my message out,
In every direction.

If a sentence is a thought,
Then a word is just a notion.
It'll give you an irritation,
That you cannot heal with lotion.

Unless you find a lotion,
That you can put under your skin,
Because the irritation that it will give you,
Is irritation from deep within.

It starts in your mind,
When you apply this teaching.
Then it moves through your thoughts.
It is learning, it's not preaching.

Then once you understand,
You'll inform several other people,
Who will continue the cycle,
Until we are all equal.

Because we are one,
You are me, and I am you.
I don't believe the Christians,
The Muslims, and the Jews.

They fight, and they quarrel.
There is always someone killing.
As it seems to me …
They should spend some time chilling.

If we are all God's children …
Then our enemy is our brother!
Where am I from?
Why can't we love one another?

The never ends

When the never ends …
And the light beam bends …

And you're out of friends …
And the ending ends …

In the evening time …
So you then unwind …

You then sit back …
What do you find?

The love will shine …
Your life will live …

The love will bind …
It's time to give.

See the strings?
    The puppeteer?

Way up above …
    They look down here.

They pull the strings …
    To make you dance.

They control your minds …
    You're in a trance.

Look up above …
    You'll find them there …

Cut your strings …
    If you truly dare.

When the never ends …
And the strings are cut.

You'll find the freedom,
And nothing but.

You are your only friend …
So in the end …

I am you,
As the light beam bends.

And all is one …
You are a star!

A solar system …
Is who you are!

A planet's moon …
A life in tune …

The cosmos in …
The month of June.

On an afternoon …
The oceans move.

The earth will spin,
Like a records groove.

The needle reads …
The sounds improve …

You hear them now …
It's time you choose …

They're in your head …
So listen up …

Choose right or wrong …
Is not enough.

You must choose wise …
As the time it flies …

As the never ends …
You close your eyes.

Can it be Yes it can

Do you live your life in a cage?
Are you at war with the rage?
As you re-read the book,
You have to re-flip the page.

In life is a story …
In life is a lesson …
In life there is injustice,
And there's also oppression.

Overcome evil.
    Overcome lies.
        Overcome illusion,
            And open your eyes.

Dissent is a word,
    And its meaning is useless.
To see who I am,
    First I must prove this:

I love all the world,
    And the people that are on it …
For peace to prevail,
    We will all have to want it.

I am near, so I'm close …
    I am an interstellar ghost.

I appear, and then I fade …
    To the few and the most.

I hold us all equal …
    The misses and misters.

Every creed, and every race …
    We all are brothers, and sisters.

As I elude,
    I conclude …

The vision expressed …
    Life is a mission …
        And life is a test.

And now that you're awakened …
And now, that you're free.
You were locked in a prison,
That you could not see.

And when you opened the lock,
And escaped from your cage …
You escaped from the prison.…
And escaped from the rage.

Love your brother and sister,
The universe wide …
As the time grows closer …
The evil will hide.

As we confront it with peace …
The love is released.
I proclaim the day,
That the war will then cease.

In life you don't own,
The love that is shown.
A tree was a seed,
Before it had grown.

The seed had been planted …
In not a pot, or a vase,
The seed in your mind …
Cannot be erased.

It will grow as a thought …
My soul can't be bought …
It is said that you have …
But you also have not.

I am you, you are me …
We exist, so we are we …
What is in a name?
And, who is now me?

And, you know I exist,
You know who I am.
I am the one who is you,
In the world again.

I see the fabric of time …
I see the vast sublime.
I see the love spread,
As I see the sun shine.

So I dissolve into matter,
And I elude the delusion.
The space that I inhabit,
Is the space of exclusion.

I am excluded from gravity.
I am excluded from bounds.
My spirit will exist …
Where there's a circle that's round.

I am the first and the last.
I am the universe vast.
I am the present, the future,
And also the past.

A space I inhabit,
I am here, and I am there.
You may think I've a home,
But I live in nowhere.

Many worlds I created,
With infinite life,
Sublime and supernatural
With pleasure and strife.

Many a world, many emotions,
I am sure of my devotion.
I exist to be as tranquil,
As the vast open ocean.

This example is free,
The freedom's not free.
If you have died in the war,
Then, you truly are me.

On this earth, there is a birth …
And there is also a death,
And then when you leave it,
You come back in a breath.

Or maybe you won't,
And you've completed your task.
It is all spelled out,
In the universe … vast …

In life, you can't own,
You will continue to find,
They had exploited your soul,
And also your mind.

Life your life now awake.
You are the god of your fate.
Only you can control,
What you put on your plate.

They will keep you in darkness,
While they bask in the light,
Tear down their walls,
And the night becomes bright....

I see you in me,
I am who you are ... We
My being is us,
And we are stars, you and me.

The only thing that is fact
Is that our life is intact,
Forever ... and ever,
If you look at the map.

The map has a legend,
And symbols are key.
The symbol of you,
Is a symbol of me.

And our symbol is old,
To some, it is a star.
To some, it is a seed.
To some, I am far.

To you, I am close.
The seed is a star,
I am you and you are me,
So that's who we are.

978-0-595-46643-6
0-595-46643-5

LaVergne, TN USA
23 March 2010
176822LV00003B/2/P